Amazing Animals

Orangutans

Michael De Medeiros

WEIGL PUBLISHERS INC.

Published by Weigl Publishers Inc.
350 5th Avenue, Suite 3304
New York, NY 10118-0069

Amazing Animals series ©2009
WEIGL PUBLISHERS INC.
www.weigl.com

Library of Congress Cataloging-in-
Publication Data

De Medeiros, Michael.
   Orangutans / Michael De Medeiros.
      p. cm.
   Includes index.
   ISBN 978-1-59036-966-1 (hard cover :
alk. paper) – ISBN 978-1-59036-967-8
(alk. paper)
   1. Orangutan–Juvenile literature. I.
Title.
   QL737.P96D43 2009
   599.88'3–dc22

2008003790

Editor
Heather Kissock
Design and Layout
Terry Paulhus, Kathryn Livingstone

Photograph Credits
Every reasonable effort has been made
to trace ownership and to obtain
permission to reprint copyright material.
The publishers would be pleased to
have any errors or omissions brought
to their attention so that they may be
corrected in subsequent printings.

Cover: Shutterstock; **Corbis:** page 21;
Getty Images: pages 1, 2, 3, 4, 5, 6, 7,
8, 9, 10, 11, 12L, 12R, 14, 15, 16, 17,
18, 19, 20, 23.

Printed in the United States of America
2 3 4 5 6 7 8 9 0 12 11 10 09

About This Book

This book tells you all about
orangutans. Find out where they
live and what they eat. Discover
how you can help to protect them.
You can also read about them in
myths and legends from around
the world.

Words in **bold** are explained in the
Words to Know section at the back
of the book.

 ## Useful Websites

Addresses in this book
take you to the home
pages of websites that
have information
about orangutans.

All of the Internet URLs given
in the book were valid at the
time of publication. However,
due to the dynamic nature of the
Internet, some addresses may have
changed, or sites may have ceased
to exist since publication. While the
author and publisher regret any
inconvenience this may cause
readers, no responsibility for any
such changes can be accepted by
either the author or the publisher.

Contents

Meet the Orangutan

Orangutans live on the Southeast Asian islands of Borneo and Sumatra. They are short, furry, playful, and smart animals. Orangutans are sometimes called red apes because they have reddish hair on their bodies.

Like humans, orangutans are primates. Primates are **mammals** that have developed hands, feet, and a large brain. Orangutans are also herbivores. This means that they eat mainly plants.

▶ As primates, orangutans share many features with humans.

Orangutan Facts

- Orangutans belong to the great ape family, which includes gorillas, chimpanzees, bonobos, and humans.

- There are two types of orangutan. They are the Bornean and Sumatran. Each type is named after the island where it lives.

▲ Orangutans can live up to 40 years in nature.

A Very Special Animal

Orangutans are one of the most intelligent animals in nature. They are able to remember where and when certain foods are available. They are also able to use items as tools to help them find food.

▼ An orangutan's thumb is much smaller than its fingers. This sometimes makes it difficult to keep a grip on small objects.

When searching for food, orangutans move around their forest **habitat** by swinging on trees. They can do this because they have very long arms and **opposable thumbs**. An orangutan's hands are shaped like hooks, making them perfect for swinging from branch to branch.

Orangutans have four fingers and an opposable thumb.

Orangutans have good eyesight. They can see in color.

An orangutan's back teeth are strong enough to crush nutshells.

An orangutan's jaws open wide enough for them to carry large items in their mouth.

An orangutan's fingers have fingerprints. These ridges help them feel and hang onto objects.

An orangutan's toes are long and **prehensile**. This helps them grasp objects.

Long Calls

To let other animals know that they are in the area, adult male orangutans send what is known as a long call. This deep, booming call sounds like the roar of a lion. A long call can be heard more than 1 mile (1.6 kilometers) away.

The long call is often used to scare away other orangutans, especially males. It can also be used to invite orangutans closer. Adult females that do not have babies hear the long call and know that an adult male is nearby. They take the call as a sign that the male wants to mate.

▶ A long call can last up to two minutes.

Orangutan Talk

- Orangutans have large **throat sacs**. The air held in these sacs gives extra force to the long calls. This force is what makes the calls so strong.

- Orangutans can make up to 15 different **vocal** sounds.

What Orangutans Eat

Most of an orangutan's diet comes from the trees in the rain forests where the animals live. Even though orangutans eat a variety of plants, their favorite food is fruit. They especially like durian. This is a yellow, football-sized fruit that tastes like butter-almond ice cream.

Besides fruit, orangutans eat leaves, mushrooms, bark, insects, eggs, termites, flowers, and nuts. They get most of their water from the food they eat, but they sometimes drink small amounts of water on its own.

▶ The orangutan's sharp front teeth are useful for tearing into large, tough-skinned fruits, such as durian.

What a Meal!

- Scientists have counted more than 400 different types of plants that orangutans eat.

- Orangutans are the largest mammal to eat a mainly fruit diet. More than half of their diet is made up of fruit.

- Orangutans like to nap after each meal.

▲ Bananas grow throughout Borneo and Sumatra, making them a popular food choice for orangutans.

Where Orangutans Live

In nature, orangutans are found only in the tropical rain forests of Borneo and Sumatra. They spend most of their time in the trees, high above the forest floor.

Orangutans even sleep in the trees. They build nests out of branches and leaves on the top of the trees and use the nests to sleep. Orangutans like to move from place to place, so they have a nest in a different tree almost every night.

▶ Sumatran orangutans have thin faces and orange beards.

▶ Bornean orangutans usually have less fur and a square-shaped face.

Orangutan Range

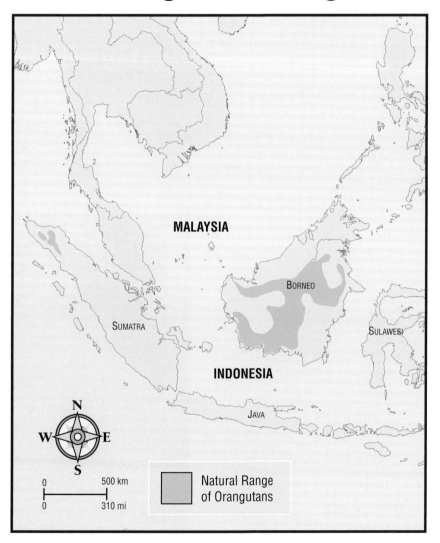

MALAYSIA

BORNEO

SUMATRA

SULAWESI

INDONESIA

JAVA

N
W E
S

| 0 | 500 km |
| 0 | 310 mi |

Natural Range
of Orangutans

Growing Up

An orangutan baby is usually born in its mother's nest. Its body is covered with red hair. Pink patches of skin circle its eyes and mouth. The baby weighs about 4 pounds (1.8 kilograms) at birth. For the first three to four years of life, an orangutan does not leave its mother's side. It depends on its mother for everything.

▼ Infants hang onto their mother's fur while she is moving.

At about age three or four, the young orangutan begins to take care of itself. It starts to move around on its own and tries to find food. By age five, the orangutan is starting to build its own nests. Childhood ends by the time the orangutan reaches seven or eight years of age.

Growth Chart

Birth	4 to 5 pounds (1.8 to 2.3 kg)	The orangutan relies on its mother's milk.
1 year old	15 pounds (6.8 kg)	The orangutan starts to eat bits of plant food.
5 years old	20 to 70 pounds (9 to 32 kg)	The orangutan learns to build its own nests.
7 to 10 years old	44 to 110 pounds (20 to 50 kg)	Childhood ends, but the orangutan remains close to its mother.
15 years old	70 to 250 pounds (31 to 113 kg)	Male and female orangutans are fully grown.

▲ Mothers carefully clean and groom their young.

Friends and Enemies

Orangutans share the rain forests with many animals, including clouded leopards, Asian elephants, and birds called hornbills. These animals sometimes compete with each other for food, but there is usually enough for everyone to get what they need.

Humans are the orangutan's main threat. People are cutting down the trees in the rain forests where the orangutans live. The trees are used for buildings, and the land is used for farming. This is leaving the orangutan with no place to live.

▼ The clouded leopard is named after the "cloudy" spots on its coat.

Useful Websites

www.orangutan.com

Click on "orangutan" at this website to learn more about the other animals orangutans live with.

Living with Orangutans

There are many different animals that live in the same places as orangutans.

- clouded leopards
- crocodiles
- elephants
- mongooses
- rhinoceroses
- tigers

▲ Like the orangutan, hornbills live in rain forests and feed on fruit.

Under Threat

There are far fewer orangutans living in nature than there were 10 years ago. They are an **endangered** animal. People are taking steps to protect the orangutan from **extinction**.

In the past 20 years, orangutans have lost up to 80 percent of their forest habitat.

Loss of habitat is the main reason for the lower **population**. People are also taking baby orangutans from their mothers to have as pets. In other cases, orangutans are used as food.

Useful Websites

www.orangutans-sos.org

Visit this website to learn about how people are trying to help save orangutans.

▲ Wildlife groups in Borneo and Sumatra work to keep the orangutans healthy. Feeding platforms in rain forests give the orangutans a place to go for food.

What Do You Think?

There are many orangutans in zoos all over the world. Zoos can make sure that the animal stays safe, but they also take them away from their natural habitat. Should orangutans be kept in **captivity**? Should they be free in their natural habitat?

Myths and Legends

Legends about orangutans often show how the animal is related to humans. In fact, the word "orangutan" comes from two Southeast Asian words. *Orang* means "person," and *hutan* means "forest." This shows that, throughout time, people have noticed how humans and orangutans are alike.

Some tales state that orangutans were once humans. In one legend, the gods punished bad people by covering them with red hair and sending them to live in the forest. These people became orangutans.

▶ Many legends are about how orangutans act like humans.

Another legend says that orangutans were a project that went wrong. When the gods first made a man and a woman, they were very proud of their work. They wanted to make another pair but could not remember how. When they tried to create more people, they made orangutans instead.

▼ The Dayak people of Borneo believe that orangutans are ghosts, not animals.

Quiz

1. Where do orangutans live in nature?
(a) **Southeast Asia** (b) **Africa** (c) **North America**

2. How long can orangutans live in nature?
(a) **20 years** (b) **30 years** (c) **40 years**

3. What do orangutans mainly eat?
(a) **meat and plants** (b) **plants** (c) **meat**

4. Where do orangutans spend most of their time?
(a) **on the forest floor** (b) **in caves** (c) **in treetops**

5. What is the orangutan's favorite fruit?
(a) **pomegranate** (b) **durian** (c) **puwin**

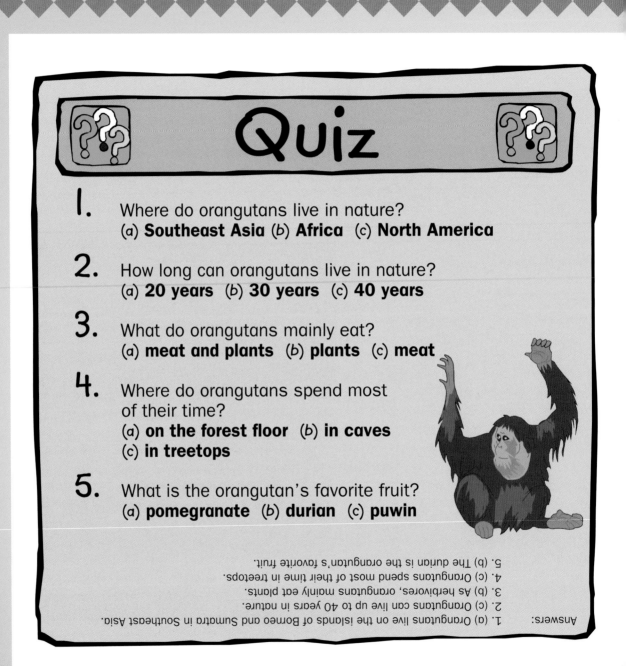

Answers:
1. (a) Orangutans live on the islands of Borneo and Sumatra in Southeast Asia.
2. (c) Orangutans can live up to 40 years in nature.
3. (b) As herbivores, orangutans mainly eat plants.
4. (c) Orangutans spend most of their time in treetops.
5. (b) The durian is the orangutan's favorite fruit.

Find out More

To find out more about orangutans, visit the websites in this book. You can also write to these organizations.

Orangutan Foundation International
4201 Wilshire Blvd. Suite 407
Los Angeles, CA 90010

International Primate Protection League
P.O. Box 766
Summerville, SC 29484

World Wildlife Fund
United States
1250 24th Street NW
Washington, DC 20037

Words to Know

captivity
the state of being confined

endangered
at risk of no longer living on Earth

extinction
the state of no longer living on Earth

habitat
the natural environment in which animals and plants live

mammals
animals that have hair or fur and feed milk to their young

opposable thumbs
special thumbs to help hold objects

population
the total number of people or animals living in a place

prehensile
specially made for gripping objects

throat sacs
the part of an orangutan's body that gathers air to make long calls

vocal
from the voice

Index